THE WILD WORLD OF ANIMALS

THE WILD WORLD OF ANIMALS

LIONS

AARON FRISCH

CREATIVE EDUCATION

Published by Creative Education. 123 South Broad Street, Mankato, Minnesota 56001. Creative Education is an imprint of The Creative Company. Designed by Rita Marshall. Production design by Advertising & Design, Inc. Photographs by akg-images / Electa, Alamy (Pat Bennett, blickwinkel, BRUCE COLEMAN INC., FLPA, Mike Hill, ImageState, Cliff Keeler, Michael Knowles, Steve Bloom Images, Stock Connection Distribution), Getty Images (Adrian Bailey, Eric Meola, Manoj Shah, Paul Souders, James Warwick), The Granger Collection, New York (pages 22-23). Copyright © 2007 Creative Education. International copyright reserved in all countries. No part of this book may be reproduced in any form without written permission from the publisher. Printed in the United States of America. Library of Congress Cataloging-in-Publication Data: Frisch, Aaron. Lions / by Aaron Frisch. p. cm. — (The wild world of animals). Includes bibliographical references. ISBN-13: 978-1-58341-433-0. 1. Lions—Juvenile literature. I. Title. II. Wild world of animals (Creative Education). QL737.C23F75 2006 599.757—dc22 2005048231. First edition 9 8 7 6 5 4 3 2 1

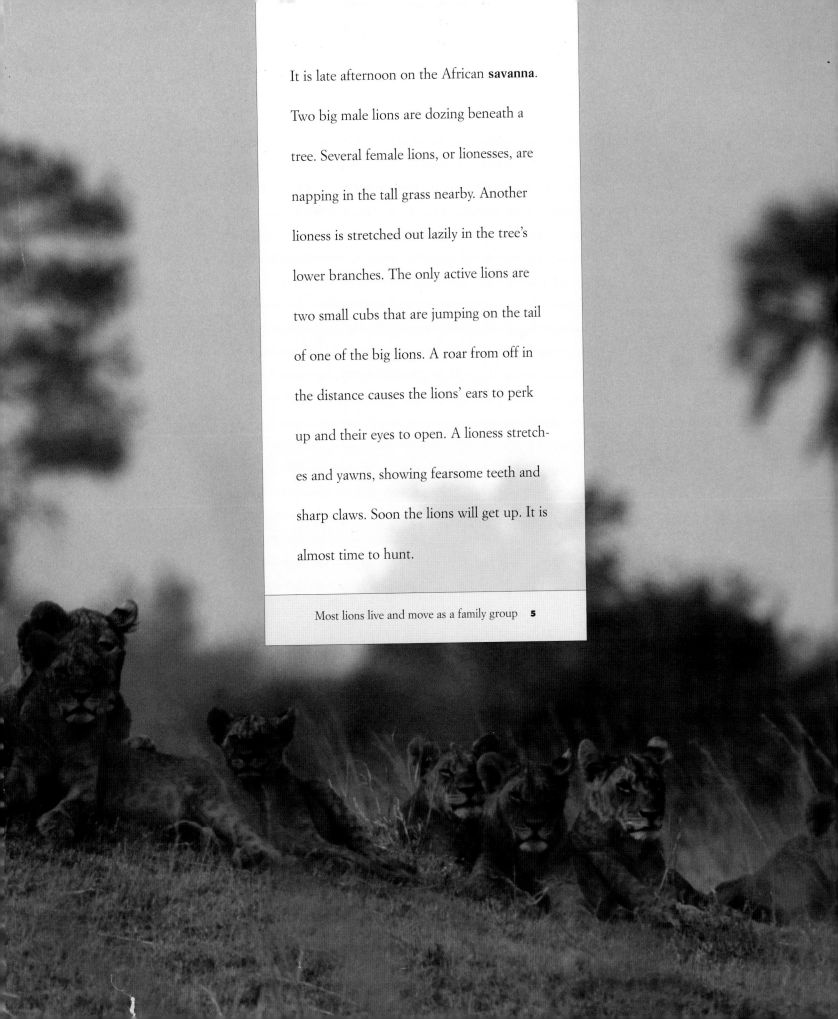

It is late afternoon on the African **savanna**. Two big male lions are dozing beneath a tree. Several female lions, or lionesses, are napping in the tall grass nearby. Another lioness is stretched out lazily in the tree's lower branches. The only active lions are two small cubs that are jumping on the tail of one of the big lions. A roar from off in the distance causes the lions' ears to perk up and their eyes to open. A lioness stretches and yawns, showing fearsome teeth and sharp claws. Soon the lions will get up. It is almost time to hunt.

Most lions live and move as a family group **5**

KING OF BEASTS

Lions are the second-biggest cats in the world, behind only tigers. Male lions are about nine feet (2.7 m) long from their nose to the tip of their tail and can weigh up to 500 pounds (227 kg)—almost as much as three men put together. Lionesses are smaller and leaner. They usually weigh less than 300 pounds (136 kg).

6   A full-grown male lion is heavy and powerful

Lions have a broad head, muscular body, and big paws. Most males have a mane that grows around their neck and shoulders and makes them look even bigger. Lionesses do not grow manes. Lions can growl, hiss, woof, and roar. A lion's roar is one of the loudest sounds in the animal kingdom. It can be heard five miles (8 km) away!

Lions are powerful animals built for hunting. A male lion's shoulders and front legs are so strong that it can kill or cripple animals such as antelopes and hyenas with a single blow. Lions have long, dagger-like claws. They also have sharp teeth perfect for tearing meat.

Lions' teeth may be three inches (7.5 cm) long   **9**

Almost all lions live on the African savanna. The savanna is mostly open grassland, but lions sometimes find shade from the hot sun under thorny trees and brush or in rocky areas. A small number of lions also live in India. Lions that live there are called Asiatic lions. They look much like African lions, but they have shorter manes.

Lions are well-suited for life on the
savanna. Except for small patches of black
fur on their ears and the tip of their tail,
lions are yellow to brownish in color. This
helps them blend in with the grass and
brush that covers the savanna and makes it
easier for them to sneak up on **prey**. Lions
have gold-colored eyes that see very well in
the dark. This is important because lions
do much of their hunting at night.

12   A hunting lion blends in with its grassy home

The African savanna is home to many large animals besides lions, including giraffes, elephants, zebras, wildebeests, and antelopes. Leopards, hyenas, and cheetahs compete with lions for food. Crocodiles live along rivers, and ostriches, warthogs, and many smaller animals and birds add to the colorful variety of life. Because a grown lion is Africa's strongest **predator** and fears no other animal, it is sometimes called the "king of beasts."

Lions share the savanna with giraffes and zebras **13**

LIFE AS A LION

Most cats are **solitary** animals, but lions live in large groups called prides. A pride usually includes a few adult males and up to a dozen lionesses and cubs. Each pride has its own **territory**, where it hunts and drinks water. Lions announce ownership of a territory by roaring and squirting a strong-smelling liquid along the edges of the territory.

14 A lion pride's territory may cover many miles

Lions mate at any time of the year, and females give birth to as many as six cubs about four months later. Cubs are born with brown spots, which help them hide in the brush when their mother is not around. Growing cubs learn by following their mother and watching her as she hunts.

16 A lioness is very protective of her young cubs

Only a few grown males can rule a pride, so young males are forced out of the pride when they are about three years old. They wander on their own or in small groups until they are strong enough to challenge a grown male for ownership of a pride. Male lions fight violently during these clashes, and the loser may be killed. Female lions stay in the same pride their entire lives.

Male lions battle to take over prides and win mates **17**

Thousands of years ago, lions lived in southern Europe, much of Asia, and all of Africa. But as humans took over these places, the **environment** changed. Lions had a harder time finding food, so they sometimes killed **livestock**. Out of fear, people then killed the lions. Sometimes people also shot or speared lions for the skin or as a way of proving their bravery.

Africa is one of the few wild places left for lions   **27**

Today, Asiatic lions are **endangered**. Only about 200 live in a corner of western India called the Gir Forest. No one is sure exactly how many African lions remain in the wild, but estimates range from 6,000 to 30,000. Most African lions live in wildlife **reserves** such as Serengeti National Park, which is in the country of Tanzania.

Lions cannot be shot in these reserves, and laws allow only a small number of lions to be hunted outside of reserves. But many lions are today "hunted" by people carrying cameras. Lions have become popular tourist attractions and are sometimes followed by small trucks carrying people excited to see African animals in the wild. This tourism does not really bother the lions, which generally ignore the people. In fact, it is a positive sign, for it will take the support and admiration of people for these magnificent cats to continue to find space to roam the savanna.

Lions are today symbols of the African wilderness **31**

GLOSSARY

The rotting meat of dead animals is called **carrion**.

An **endangered** animal is one that is at risk of dying off so that it no longer exists on Earth.

An animal's surroundings are called its **environment**.

An animal that is stabbed with another animal's horn or tusk is said to be **gored**.

Livestock are the horses, cattle, sheep, or other animals raised on farms or ranches.

A **predator** is an animal that kills and eats other animals.

Prey animals are animals that are caught and eaten by other animals.

Reserves are areas of land set aside to provide a place for animals to live.

A **savanna** is a plain in a hot, mostly dry area; it has tall grass and scattered trees.

Scavengers are animals such as vultures and hyenas that eat the remains of dead animals.

Solitary animals spend most of their time by themselves or with just their young.

A **territory** is an area an animal claims for its own.

BOOKS

Denis-Huot, Christine and Michael. *The Lion: King of the Beasts.* Watertown, Mass.: Charlesbridge Publishing, 2000.

Dineen, Jacqueline. *Lions.* North Mankato, Minn.: Smart Apple Media, 2003.

Kalman, Bobbie, and Amanda Bishop. *The Life Cycle of a Lion.* New York: Crabtree Publishing, 2002.

WEB SITES

Kids Planet: African Lion http://www.kidsplanet.org/factsheets/african_lion.html

National Geographic.com Kids http://www.nationalgeographic.com/kids/creature_feature/0109/lions.html

World Almanac for Kids: Lion http://www.worldalmanacforkids.com/explore/animals/lion.html

INDEX